A Young Shepherd

A Young Shepherd

Cat Urbigkit

Boyds Mills Press

Text copyright © 2006 by Cat Urbigkit
All rights reserved

Published by Boyds Mills Press, Inc.
A Highlights Company
815 Church Street
Honesdale, Pennsylvania 18431
Printed in China

CIP data is available

First edition, 2006
The text of this book is set in 14-point Wilke Roman.

Visit our Web site at www.boydsmillspress.com

10 9 8 7 6 5 4 3 2 1

To the Bill Thoman family, who launched my family
into the sheep business with orphan lambs
—C. U.

Cass lives on a sheep ranch in Wyoming. The ranch is called Paradise Sheep Company.

Cass, who is twelve, has his own flock of sheep, but like all good shepherds, he helps care for all the sheep on his family's ranch.

Cass started his herd by buying some "bum" lambs from friends who also have a sheep ranch. Bum lambs are orphans, meaning that they have lost their mothers for some reason. So Cass has to take care of the bums, providing them with three main things: water, food, and shelter.

The first thing Cass has to do is put the lambs in a safe, sheltered place with plenty of hay for the lambs to bed down in and heat to keep them warm. Newborn lambs need food energy as well, so they need to be fed small amounts of special milk every few hours. Ewe's milk is best, but powdered milk replacer works fine, also.

Abe, Cass's herding dog, goes with Cass to feed the lambs.

Cass carefully mixes the powder with hot water, and then pours it into a bottle. When a rubber nipple is put on the top, the lamb bottle is ready to go.

Cass, with help from his parents, will bottle-feed each of these lambs until they grow big enough to drink from a special bucket. This usually takes only a few weeks.

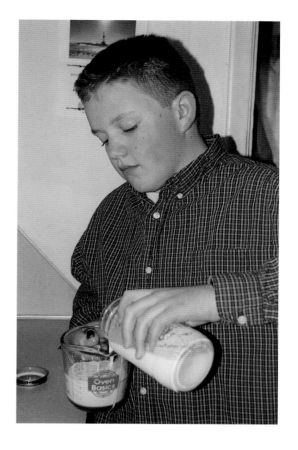

When the lambs graduate to the bucket, feeding time is much faster and easier for Cass. He pours the milk mixture into the bucket, and then hangs the bucket on a fence, where up to four lambs can drink together at one time.

Although the lambs are still too young to rely on hay, they nibble on it, along with grass and everything else! Cass always leaves fresh hay and grain available for them as well as fresh water.

Like other babies, lambs sleep a lot, but they also like to play. They race each other, leap in the air, and jump on anything they can.

Jordan is one of Cass's ewes. Cass named her Jordan because when she was little, she could jump very high, reminding Cass of one of his favorite basketball players, Michael Jordan.

Pretty Eyes is another one of the ewes Cass named. Even though she's all grown up now, she still has pretty eyes.

Sheep are social animals, so lambs always seem to grow better and are healthier if they are raised together rather than alone.

Sheep also need protection from predators, and Cass's family uses guardian dogs to protect their herd. Cass lets the guardian dog pups bed down in his bum lamb pen, and friendships begin quickly. This process is called bonding.

Cass bonds with his lambs as well, visiting with them and taking them out of their pen to play. The lambs become used to being touched and handled, making some of the tasks Cass has to do later much easier.

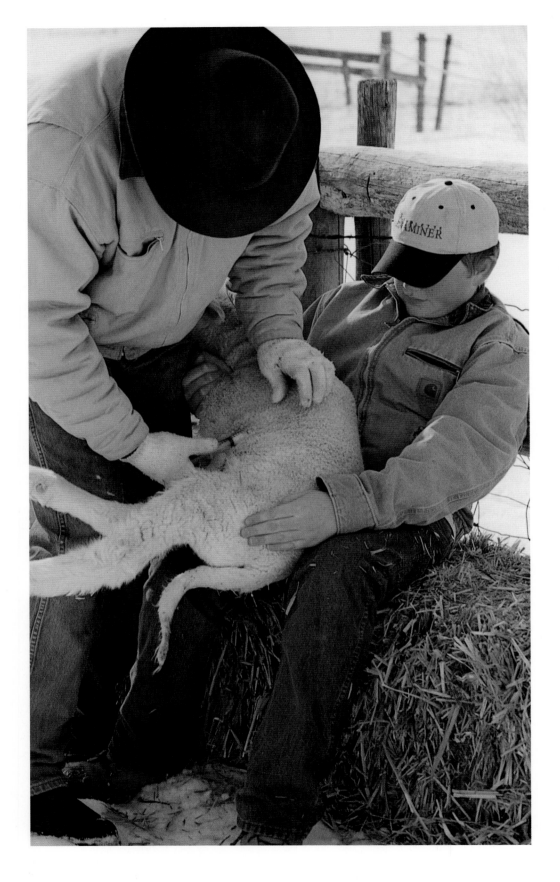

Lambs, like children, need to be vaccinated against certain diseases that could make them very ill or even kill them. When the lambs are a few months old, Cass and his dad give each lamb a shot, protecting them against these diseases.

Another job that must be done is docking the lambs' tails. Those long wiggly tails are cute now, but as the lambs grow, their tails can become contaminated with manure, which can eventually make the sheep sick.

Sheep ranchers "dock" the lambs' tails, which means to cut the tail off. Sometimes a sharp knife is used, but Cass uses small, strong rubber bands on his lambs' tails. The bands are put in place with a tool called a ring expander. The bands stop the blood flow to the tail, causing the tail to fall off within a few weeks.

Even though Cass is still feeding the lambs milk in a bucket, they go out during the day to meet the other sheep in the herd and to play.

As the lambs stay out more and more with the herd, they eat more grass, so Cass feeds them less milk. By the time the lambs are three months old, Cass quits providing them milk. This process is called weaning.

Now that the lambs have become full-time members of the herd, Cass catches his lambs to place ear tags in their ears.

Each tag has its own number, which Cass carefully records. This way, he'll always know which sheep are his.

He also writes down other information about each lamb, including when it was born, what vaccinations it's had, and other important data.

Cass is a member of a 4-H club, and he decided to show some of his bum lambs in the county fair. To get ready for the fair, Cass had to carefully wash and groom his lambs, as well as enter information about his lambs' nutrition and growth in his record book.

It was all worth it, as Cass and his lambs had a great time at the county fair.

His lambs looked nice and earned purple ribbons, while Cass had a good experience in learning how to show his livestock for the judge and in front of an audience.

With show season over, the rest of the year was easier for Cass. His lambs stayed with the herd, growing and doing well, and Cass checked them every day, sometimes while riding his horse, Indian.

Often, Abe went along as well.

In the fall, Cass helped his parents pick out a new ram to bring into the herd. The rams will be turned out with the ewe flock in December and will be the fathers of the lambs born five months later in May.

During the winter, the sheep herd is fed hay every day and their wool grows long. Cass and his dad walk through the herd, handling several sheep to check their wool and to be sure the animals are staying healthy and in good condition.

In April, a month before lambing, it's time to shear. A professional sheep shearer, Brent Flower, visits the ranch, carefully shearing all the sheep in the herd.

Cass helps by sorting the wool and operating the baler. Later, the wool will be sold and used to make clothing.

May is exciting because that's when the ewes give birth to their lambs. Every two hours, Cass or one of his parents walk through the herd to see if any new lambs have been born or to assist any ewe needing help in lambing. If it's cold at night, the sheep can be moved into the barn to have their babies.

Some of the lambs Cass raised are now adult ewes, having their own lambs. Because he handled and cared for the ewes when they were young, they trust him to be gentle with their new babies.

It makes Cass very happy that his orphan lambs grew up to be such good mothers. It also means that his herd continues to grow, as more lambs are born to his flock.

NOTE

There are more than two hundred breeds of domestic sheep in the world, with some valued for their meat, and others for their wool. In the United States, Texas is the leading sheep-producing state, followed by California. Wyoming, where Cass lives, comes in third. Sheep are great youth projects. It's relatively inexpensive to start a sheep herd; sheep are smaller and easier to handle than large species like cattle; and kids can do most of the work themselves. Here are five common sheep breeds that would make good youth projects.

Finnsheep: Finnsheep, which originated in Finland, is a breed that has multiple litters of lambs rather than the more typical one or two. Four to six lambs are not uncommon. Finnsheep are well suited to rugged environments and thrive in cold Wyoming winters. Laney Johnston, eleven, demonstrates how easy it is for her to handle a Finn ewe.

Targhee: The Targhee is an American breed developed at the United States Sheep Experiment Station in Idaho. Targhee is the name of the national forest on which the station's sheep graze. Targhee ewes are large, fine-wooled, and have a high percentage of twin and triplet lambs. Cody David, fifteen, has owned his own Targhee flock for four years, thanks to a youth flock program sponsored by the Wyoming Wool Growers Association.

Rambouillet: Cass raises Rambouillet sheep, a breed that originated in France but is now the most common breed in commercial range flocks in the western United States. Rambouillets are valued for both their meat production and their wool production, with about 10 pounds of wool harvested from each ewe every year. This breed is also known for its strong flocking instinct, which helps protect the animals against predation.

Suffolk: This English breed is characterized by its black ears, face, and legs that are wool-free. Suffolks are a meat breed that experiences rapid growth. Emily Johnston, twelve, crosses her Suffolks with Rambouillets to get a fast-growing meat sheep with medium-quality wool.

Dorset: The Dorset is a breed that originated in England and has lightweight wool that is treasured for hand spinning. Twin lambs are a characteristic of this breed, which may lamb as often as twice a year. Shelby Reneau, eight, has helped her family with their sheep for several years.